MW00594294

This book belongs to:

____

Made in the USA
Middletown, DE
01 March 2023

25986196R00066